LIBERTY

We would like to thank the many local people who have contributed to this book and these images.

ISSN 978-0-9930809-2-0

First published in England 2018
Published by Deptford Heritage Publishing.

Design, print and production by Typecast Colour Ltd, Paddock Wood TN12 6DQ

Email : raymondwoolford@aol.com

 Ray_Woolford

. . . .
This work made possible thanks to:
• Playwright Dr Tom Band
• Scottish Historian George Proudfoot
• The National Archive
• The British Library
• The House of Commons
• Marx Library
• The People's Archive Manchester
• Greenwich Heritage Centre Archive.

Deptford Radical History and the Peasant's Revolt first published in Deptford a radical history
by Ray Barron-Woolford ISBN number 879-0-9930809-0-6

LIBERTY

A New Play

By Ray Barron-Woolford

"DISTURBER OF THE PEACE"

WOMAN'S REFUSAL TO BE BOUND OVER

At the Tower Bridge Police Court yesterday KATH DUNCAN, 44, married, of Ommaney Road, New Cross, appeared on a warrant which alleged that "On December 14, 1932, she was a disturber of the peace of our Lord the King and an inciter of others to commit crimes and misdemeanours, and as such is subject to the provisions of the Statute of 34 Edward III."

Mr. E. Clayton, solicitor, on behalf of the Director of Public Prosecutions, said the subject of complaint was in some words used by Duncan on December 14 in a speech she made at the Bermondsey Town Hall, at a meeting of the National Unemployed Workers' Movement. It was a speech calculated to create a breach of the peace, and the defendant seemed to have taken a very prominent part, and she repeated these words at subsequent meetings as well. The words she used were:—" The Public Assistance people should be held personally responsible. [Mr. Clayton said he thought Duncan was then speaking about a Bermondsey murder case.] The Public Assistance people should be identified and their addresses found, in order that pressure could be brought to bear on them. It is the duty of the workers to do this. Every member of a local Public Assistance Committee who refuses relief to unemployed men or who wants to send an unemployed man to Belmont, must be identified and addresses got, so that they can be intimidated."

Mr. Clayton said that the Director considered that those words were calculated to provoke a breach of the peace, and there was no doubt that Duncan had personally endeavoured to carry out these threats.

Detective-Inspector Jones, of the Special Branch, said he was at the meeting in question and heard Duncan use the words alleged. He did not take a shorthand note, but made a note soon after.

Mr. CAMPION (the magistrate), after examining the officer's notebook, said:—" I see you have been merciful to this woman. Besides what you have given in evidence, I see you have got in your note : ' These people are not necessarily local and can walk about, under the new law, without being hissed, booed, or spat upon by the workers.' "

Detective-sergeant Phillips said he saw Duncan at a demonstration in Hollydale Road, Peckham, on December 16 outside the works of Mr. Evan Cook, a borough councillor. The demonstrators used filthy and insulting words. They then went to Camberwell Town Hall, where they were refused admission.

Duncan, in a long, rambling speech, denied that she had used any inciting words or conduct likely to provoke a breach of the peace. She said she had been a public worker for five years and would not do anything so foolish.

Mr. CAMPION said he would be willing to take Duncan's word that no such conduct would happen again, and would bind her over in her own recognizances to keep the peace for six months.

Duncan.—What if I refuse ?

Mr. CAMPION.—You will have to find a surety in £50.

Duncan.—I do not want any sureties.

Mr. CAMPION.—It is obvious to me that you do not intend to keep the peace. You refuse to promise me ?

Duncan.—I cannot accept your interpretation. What is the alternative ?

Mr. CAMPION.—I shall order you to find a surety in £50 to keep the peace for six months, or you will go to prison for one month in default.

Duncan refused to find a surety and was removed to Holloway Prison to serve the sentence of imprisonment in default.

Contents

LABOUR BAN ON MEETINGS

Kath Duncan Arrested At Task Work Centre

Comrade Kath Duncan, of Deptford, was arrested at the Nynehead Street test and task work centre yesterday, for obstructing the police. She will be charged at Tower Bridge Police Court this morning.

She was speaking at a meeting held under the auspices of the National Unemployed Workers' Movement and the Council of Civil Liberties, to

KATH DUNCAN

break the ban which has been placed on meetings by the Labour L.C.C.

Regular meetings have been held at this spot during the last two years, but now the police say they have instructions from the supervisor to stop all

Kath Duncan

Kath Duncan was a legendary communist activist in Deptford in the 1930s. A teacher, she became a redoubtable organiser of the unemployed. She was a powerful orator and a woman with obvious personal magnetism and an attractive demeanour. The local Deptford press felt unable to refer to her without mentioning her "blazing red hair"!

Katherine Duncan was born around 1889 in Scotland, a descendent, she claimed, of Rob Roy, who "would never steal from the poor". In her youth she was much influenced by the suffragette movement and joined the Independent Labour Party in her village.

A teacher and member of the NUT, in 1923 she moved to Hackney in London with her husband, Sandy, who was also a teacher. There they joined both the local Independent Labour Party and the Hackney Labour Dramatic Group. Husband and wife remained ILP members until the 1926 general strike, when they joined the Communist Party.

In 1929 Kath was elected to the party's Central Committee for one term.

Kath and Sandy moved to Deptford in 1930. Soon afterwards, Kath threw herself into work on behalf of the National Unemployed Workers Movement, becoming a powerful and prolific street orator. A small woman who made powerful speeches, she organised deputations of the unemployed to the Deptford Urban District Council offices that were often 5,000 strong. Alf Lucas, the Deptford NUWM organiser would often speak at these events.

Kath herself headed one such mammoth local deputation, which specifically demanded action to clear the slums and provide work. Children on the march held posters saying: "Daddy's on the Dole". Such was the size of the deputation that the Council was forced to suspend its standing orders.

In 1931, Kath Duncan stood as a communist in the parliamentary elections for the Greenwich constituency.

During May and June of 1932, hundreds of workers frequently marched to the docks (often through the Blackwell tunnel) to urge dockers not to load "murder ships" with military equipment destined for Japan, which was then in the process of invading mainland China.

On one Sunday in June, 1932, a group of marchers returning from a 3,000-strong meeting in Woolwich, at which Kath and Sandy had spoken, were informed by a police inspector that they must stop singing the 'Red Flag'. When they refused, a large number of police appeared and laid into the crowd with batons. They arrested many of the marchers, including Alf Lucas.

Deptford Broadway, back in the day.

The Broadway Theatre, on the corner of Deptford High Street and the Broadway (1930s).

Sandy Duncan was hospitalised and the events became known locally as the "Battle of Deptford Broadway".

The news of this unprovoked attack was met with great indignation in Deptford. The next day, as a direct result of the police attack, unemployed men at the Unemployed Training Centre went on strike. An eight-thousand-strong crowd gathered on Deptford Broadway, where Kath demanded the dismissal of the inspector. The police responded with a mounted police charge, batons raining down on the crowd.

On Tuesday, the Daily Worker reported "groups of police patrolling about and the place is liked an armed camp". Later, pictures of those arrested were sold to raise money for the "defence fund". Some were released in early October. Two of those jailed, Albert Crane, a 24-year-old hosiery worker, and George Childs, a 24-year old clerk, were met by "a small band of Deptford Communists" on their release from Brixton prison, and went on to address a meeting of 400 people on Deptford Broadway where they "said they would not be afraid to go back if there was any chance of it doing any good to the working classes of Deptford".

These children marched in a South Wales demonstration against the Means Test and the new scales

Six months after the main events, on 19th December 1932, Kath appeared in court, under laws originally used against the leaders of the 14th-century peasant revolt, on a charge of being "a disturber of the Peace of our Lord the King". She refused to be bound over or stay out of politics, and was sentenced to six months in Holloway Prison. (Coincidentally, the 76-year-old Tom Mann was in Brixton Prison at the same time for the very same reason!) While in prison, Kath was forced to make shirts which she herself was "convinced no one would wear".

On her release the people of Deptford flocked to greet her on the Broadway. However the LCC Education Committee wrote to her a few days after her release to inform her they were going to remove her from the list of approved London County Council teachers. A campaign opposing the attempted victimisation and spearheaded by the NUT and other unions secured 5,700 signatures in Deptford alone, and as a result the attempt to remove her was defeated.

By 1932, Kath was the acknowledged leader of the unemployed in Deptford, and her open-air meetings had become a feature of political life in South East London. She spoke on platforms with the NUWM leader, Wal Hannington, and at a major

The White Swan Inn in Loving Edward Lane (now Edward Street) (1819). It was the house in which the Police Courts were held prior to the establishment of the Greenwich Police Court in 1840. It was also a staging post for the stage coach to Charing Cross. The Old Red Cow Inn (next door but one) marks the site of the old toll house before it was moved to Evelyn Street in 1834.

NUWM rally in Hyde Park in February 1933. She was involved in securing accommodation in Deptford for unemployed marchers from Kent on their way to Hyde Park in October 1932 and, two years later, for 30 unemployed marchers from Scotland.

Kath and the NUWM South East London organiser, Vic Parker, stood as communist candidates in the 1934 LCC elections. She recalled how a bunch of red carnations arrived at the Communist Party committee rooms at Tanners Hill, sent with best wishes from the boys at Surrey Commercial Docks. Kath appreciated the gesture greatly as dockers had once thrown "ochre", a red dye, over her.

In 1935, Kath, now living at Ommaney Road, New Cross, was once again arrested for refusing to move her meeting from outside the local Unemployment Training

Centre at Nynehead Street, New Cross, when asked to do so by Police Inspector William Jones. This provided the first test case for the National Council for Civil Liberties, now known as Liberty, which had been founded in 1934 at a time when workers' protests were subject to severe civil-liberty constraints. As disturbances had occurred at a similar meeting over a year earlier, Jones claimed that he was duty bound to prevent it happening again. But this potentially created a precedent that would allow the police to ban any political meeting in public places at will, simply by expressing a fear of disorder.

Not only was Duncan v. Jones [1936] the first case taken up by the NCCL, it was a landmark in the law on public order. Despite representation from D. N. Pritt K.C. and Mr Dingle Foot MP, Kath Duncan was fined 40 shillings and costs of five guineas. But her case had gone down in legal history: Kath had been about to make a public address, in a situation similar to one in which, a year before, a disturbance had been incited by her speaking, when she was stopped by the police on the grounds that she would destabilise civil peace by the strength of her words. Even though Kath was arrested while peacefully speaking to a small crowd, she was charged with police obstruction.

This raised the question not of the quality of her conduct but of the reasonableness of the constable's understanding of it. What the constable had to evaluate was the reality of the risk of a breach of the peace.

The Chief Justice's judgment at the end of the trial made it clear that the much-vaunted British democracy, in the absence of a written constitution guaranteeing the right of free speech, is merely a construct of propaganda. His view was that "English law does not recognise any special right of public meeting for political or other purposes. The right of assembly is nothing more than a view taken by the court of the individual liberty of the subject." In other words, it all depends! Even so, for much of the rest of the last century, the practical effect of Duncan v. Jones was to support the notion that free speech was an absolute right, unless the situation was genuinely likely to get out of hand. Kath lost the case but won the war for us, at least for sixty-odd years. Of course, in recent years, as the 'war against terror' has taken priority, public order legislation has got tougher.

Kath spoke regularly about the threat of fascism and was involved in the famous Battle of Cable Street in the East End as well as the Battle of Bermondsey. On one occasion, the fascists singled Kath out for special attention but, thanks to a tip-off, local anti-fascists were able to chase them off.

Kath was heavily involved in the Aid to Spain movement, organising door-to-door collections on Sundays throughout Deptford and raising £100 towards an ambulance. She also interviewed men who wished to fight in the International Brigade in Spain. Les Stannard was considered too young to fight in Spain but he and other Deptford YCL-ers were inspired by Kath Duncan's commitment.

Sandy died in Scotland towards the end of the war and, by 1945, Kath was working for the local Labour MP, though she was now crippled by arthritis.

Around 1953, Kath's sister took her home to the Scottish village where she was born and it was here that she died in August 1954. After her death, the London District Committee of the Communist Party produced a pamphlet, "Deptford's tribute to Kath Duncan", in which the author stated: "Where there was a job to do, Kath was always with us… She would march off at the head, leading the way, full of vitality and purpose. She was always a striking and imposing figure with her neat black costume, spotless white collar, and a black, wide-brimmed straw hat, worn at an angle showing her auburn, short-cropped hair".

Deptford the place after Kilcardy Kath saw as home

A cobbled street in a Deptford slum, c. 1900

Deptford began life as a ford of the Ravensbourne (near what is now Deptford Bridge station) along the route of the Celtic trackway, which was later paved by the Romans and developed into the medieval Watling Street; it was part of the pilgrimage route from London to Canterbury used by the pilgrims in Chaucer's Canterbury Tales, and Deptford itself is mentioned in the Prologue to the "Reeve's Tale". The ford developed into a wooden and then a stone bridge, and in 1497 saw the Battle of Deptford Bridge, in which rebels from Cornwall, led by Michael An Gof, marched on London protesting against punitive taxes, but were soundly beaten by the King's forces.

A second settlement developed as a modest fishing village on the Thames until Henry VIII used that site for a royal dock for building, repairing and supplying ships, after which it grew in size and importance, shipbuilding remaining in operation until March 1869. Trinity House, the organisation concerned with the safety of navigation around the British Isles, was formed in Deptford in 1514, with its first Master being Thomas Spert, captain of the Mary Rose; it moved to Stepney in 1618. The name "Trinity House'derives from the church of the Holy Trinity and St Clement, which adjoined the dockyard.

Originally separated by market gardens and fields, the two areas merged over the years, with the docks becoming an important part of the Elizabethan exploration. Queen Elizabeth I visited the royal dockyard on 4 April 1581 to knight the adventurer Francis Drake. As well as exploration, Deptford was important for trade – the Honourable East India Company had a yard in Deptford from 1607 until late in the 17th century. It was also connected with the slave trade, John Hawkins using it as a base for his operations, and Olaudah Equiano, the slave who became an important part of the abolition of the slave trade, was sold from one ship's captain to another in Deptford around 1760.

Diarist John Evelyn lived in Deptford at Sayes Court from 1652. Evelyn inherited the house when he married the daughter of Sir Richard Browne in 1652. On his return to England at the Restoration, Evelyn laid out meticulously planned gardens in the French style, with hedges and parterres. In its grounds was a cottage at one time rented by master woodcarver Grinling Gibbons. After Evelyn had moved to Surrey in 1694,

Russian Tsar Peter the Great studied shipbuilding for three months in 1698. He and some of his fellow Russians stayed at Sayes Court, the manor house of Deptford. Evelyn was angered at the antics of the Tsar, who got drunk with his friends and, using a wheelbarrow with Peter in it, rammed their way through a fine holly hedge. Sayes Court was demolished in 1728-9 and a workhouse built on its site. Part of the estates around Sayes Court were purchased in 1742 for the building of the Admiralty Victualling Yard, renamed the Royal Victoria Yard in 1858 after a visit by Queen Victoria. This massive facility included warehouses, a bakery, a cattle yard/abattoir and sugar stores, and closed in 1960. All that remains is the name of Sayes Court Park, accessed from Sayes Court Street off Evelyn Street, not far from Deptford High Street. The Pepys Estate, opened on 13 July 1966, is on the former grounds of the Royal Victoria Dockyard.

The docks had been gradually declining since the 18th century; the new, larger ships found the Thames difficult to navigate, and Deptford was now competing with the new docks at Plymouth, Portsmouth and Chatham. When the Napoleonic Wars ended in 1815, the need for docks to build and repair warships declined; the docks shifted from shipbuilding to concentrate on victualling at the Royal Victoria Victualling Yard, and the Royal Dock closed in 1869. From 1871 until the First World War, the shipyard site was the City of London Corporation's Foreign Cattle Market, in which girls and women butchered sheep and cattle until the early part of the 20th century. At its peak, around 1907, over 234,000 animals were imported annually through the market, but by 1912 these figures had declined to less than 40,000 a year. The yard was taken over by the War Office in 1914, and was an Army Supply Reserve Depot in the First and Second World Wars. The site lay unused until it was purchased by Convoys (newsprint importers) in 1984 and eventually came into the ownership of News International. In the mid-1990s, although significant investment had been made on the site, it became uneconomic to continue using it as a freight wharf. In 2008 Hutchison Whampoa bought the 16 hectare site from News International with plans for a £700m, 3,500-home development scheme. The Grade II listed Olympia Warehouse is to be be refurbished as part of the redevelopment of the site.

Deptford experienced economic decline in the 20th century with the closing of the docks, and the damage caused by the bombing during the Second World War – a V-2 rocket destroyed a Woolworths store outside Deptford Town Hall, killing 160 people. High unemployment caused some of the population to move away as the riverside industries closed down in the late 1960s and early 1970s. The local council have developed plans with private companies to regenerate the riverside area and the town centre.

The Peasants' Revolt

The Peasant's Revolt: The last great battle between King and the people fought in Deptford the charge that led to the leaders being hung drawn and quartered the same charge Kath Duncan would be charged with again in Deptford hundreds of years later.

The Peasants' Revolt, also called Wat Tyler's Rebellion or the Great Rising, was a major uprising across large parts of England in 1381.

The revolt had various causes, including the socio-economic and political tensions generated by the Black Death in the 1340s, the high taxes resulting from the conflict with France during the Hundred Years War, and instability within the local leadership of London. The final trigger for the revolt was the intervention of a royal official, John Bampton, in Essex on 30 May 1381. His attempts to collect unpaid poll taxes in the town of Brentwood ended in a violent confrontation, which rapidly spread across the south-east of the country. People from a wide spectrum of rural society, including many local artisans and village officials, rose up in protest, burning court records and opening the local gaols. The rebels sought a reduction in taxation, an end to the system of unfree labour known as serfdom, and the removal of the King's senior officials and law courts.

Inspired by the sermons of the radical cleric John Ball and led by Wat Tyler, a contingent of Kentish rebels advanced on London. They were met at Blackheath, just yards from the site of the future Battle of Deptford Bridge, by representatives of the royal government, who unsuccessfully attempted to persuade them to return home. King Richard II, then aged only 14, retreated to the safety of the Tower of London, but most of the royal forces were abroad or in northern England. On 13 June, the rebels entered London and, joined by many local townsfolk, attacked the gaols, destroyed the Savoy Palace and the Temple Inns of Court, set fire to law books and killed anyone associated with the royal government. The following day, Richard met the rebels at Mile End and acceded to most of their demands, including the abolition of serfdom. Meanwhile, rebels entered the Tower of London, killing the Lord Chancellor and the Lord High Treasurer, whom they found inside.

On 15 June, Richard left the city to meet with Tyler and the rebels at Smithfield. Violence broke out, and Richard's party killed Tyler. Richard defused the tense situation

Richard II meets the rebels on 13 June 1381.
(Miniature from a 1470s copy of Jean Froissart's Chronicles.)

long enough for London's mayor, William Walworth, to gather a militia from the city and disperse the rebel forces. Richard immediately began to re-establish order in London and rescinded his previous grants to the rebels. The revolt had also spread into East Anglia, where the University of Cambridge was attacked and many royal officials were killed. Unrest continued until the intervention of Henry le Despenser, who defeated a rebel army at the Battle of North Walsham on 25 or 26 June. Troubles extended north to the cities of York, Beverley and Scarborough, and west as far as Bridgwater in Somerset. Richard mobilised around 4,000 soldiers to help restore order. Most of the rebel leaders were tracked down and executed; by November, at least 1,500 rebels had been killed.

The Peasants' Revolt has been widely studied by academics. Late 19th-century historians used a range of sources from contemporary chroniclers to assemble an account of the uprising, and these were supplemented in the 20th century by research using court records and local archives.

Interpretations of the revolt have shifted over the years. Once seen as a defining moment in English history, modern academics are less certain of its impact on subsequent social and economic history. The revolt heavily influenced the course of the Hundred Years War, by deterring later Parliaments from raising additional taxes to pay for military campaigns in France. The revolt has been widely used in socialist literature, including by the author William Morris, and remains a potent political symbol for the political left, informing the arguments surrounding the introduction of the Community Charge in the United Kingdom during the 1980s.

DRAMATIS PERSONAE

Kath Duncan – Political Activist

Sandy – Her Husband

Fred Copeman – Friend of Kath Duncan

Mam – Kath Duncan's Mother

Policeman 1

Police 2

Comrade 1

Comrade 2

Lodger In Kath Duncan's House

Chairman of Local Communist Party

R. Kidd – Member of CP

A Bing – Member of CP

E. Hanley – Member of CP

A Prison Governor

Warden 1

Warden 2

Speaker of The House of Commons

George Lansbury MP
Leader of The Labour Party

Frank Boyd Merriman MP (Con.)
Solicitor General

George Holford Knight MP (Lab.)

Olivier Stanley MP (Con.)

George Buchanan MP (Lab.)

Sir John Gilmour MP (Con.)
Home Secretary

Valentine Mcentee MP (Lab.)

James Maxton MP
(Independent Labour Party)

David Lloyd George MP (Lib.)
Leader Of The House

"A TERRIBLE RECORD."

DEPTFORD MAN'S CONVICTIONS.

"You have a terrible record," remarked Mrs. A. G. Mann, the chairman, at Bromley Police Court yesterday, in passing sentence of 12 months' hard labour on Henry Ward (40), a journalist, of Brookmill-road, Deptford, who was charged on remand with being a suspected person found loitering at Bromley Common on October 12th and with being a person amenable under the Prevention of Crimes Act. Charles Thomas (32), a chauffeur, of the same address, was sentenced to three months' imprisonment for being a suspected person found loitering at Bromley Common at the same time.

Twelve convictions, including two sentences of three years' penal servitude, were proved against Ward, and five convictions were proved against Thomas. It was stated that the men became acquainted in prison.

LEE WOMEN CONSERVATIVES.

The South Ward Women's branch of the East Lewisham Conservative Association and a whist drive in the hall of Lee High

LIBERTY

By Ray Barron-Woolford

Act 1 Scene 1

Kath is on her soap box on Deptford Broadway after getting back from protesting at Woolwich docks where she has led protestors lobbying dock workers to stop loading up arms for war.

Kath: Comrades, we can never stand by whilst women and children and fellow comrades pay with their lives, with weapons loaded by OUR dock workers in OUR Docks to fight another person's war. The screams of the children and the women maimed and injured along with their loved- ones killed, we can all relate to. Is there not one person among you who did not lose a loved-one in the war we were told would be the last? Comrades, I just call on you to demand what is fair and just:

The right to a fair day's pay for a fair day's work.

An end to slums, starvation and malnutrition that we all see and live with cheek by jowl.

Welfare not soup kitchens.

Education not domestic enslavement.

I stand here before you as an equal and yet, in law, I am not. We cannot say what we think, or speak what we feel for fear of the long arm of the law. What type of society will happily send us and you all to war, which allows our streets to be full of the soldiers who fought their war and return home to beg street by street, town by town for the crumbs from their lordships' tables?

In Russia today, the Russia Republic flourishes like a beacon in the darkness.

Our fellow comrades have stood and fought at the Battle of Deptford Bridge, where we now stand. This spot, Deptford Bridge, is where, in 1381, Wat Tyler led the Peasants' Revolt. In 1497 Michael An Gof led his brave Cornish workers' army to protest against the King's punitive taxes, only to be beaten by the King. Today we have another King, but this time, my comrades, we must stand firm. We must lead the fight for social justice and be united, for there is no other path to take.

Police arrive.

Police 1: You must also put down your weapons, disperse and go home.

Kath: We seek no trouble here, just to speak a just injustice and to share in solidarity with comrades and fellow workers. Our weapons are our words of truth, but the banners we carry are just that; our words. Violence plays no part in our struggle or our protest here today.

Police 2: Break up all your banners and put the poles away from us clearly in a pile.

Kath starts singing the Red Flag. Others join in.

Police 1: You will disperse and put down your weapons, or we will.

Kath and rest all singing the Red Flag

Police charge on horse-back and with batons, beating the protestors and dragging many into the back of police vans,

Kath is still singing on her soap box

Kath: (*Yells out*) Comrades! Link arms; stand firm! If the police are intent on recreating the Battle of Deptford Bridge, not one man, woman or child among you, raise an arm. Let them be the victims of their injustice.

Carries on singing Red Flag. All around her people flee. Kath alone is still the last person singing on the last chorus as a small team link arms in a circle around her, covered in blood, broken and battered.

Police leave with vans full of prisoners, Kath helps people back to her house.

Act 1 Scene 2: Back at Kath's House

Mam is in an apron with head scarf, scrubbing the front door step which is covered in blood from the people escaping into the house

Fred: Thank goodness you are OK.

Kath: Yes, Fred, but they have taken Sandy with dozens of others. Those they could not snatch, they badly beat. We need to set up a fighting fund to help those hauled off to jail and get medical care for our comrades. We need to spread the word what happened here today. This Battle of Deptford Bridge must be the last; far too much blood has been spilt on this place. No more!

Act 1 Scene 3

Public meeting in Deptford to debate what to do about number of comrades being arrested and charged for protesting or speaking out. Group of people sitting around a table with Fred and Sandy Duncan among them

Fred: Kath Duncan was amazing this week; the police say 30,000 marched with her on the Gas Works on the Old Kent Road against the fuel poverty tax.

Sandy: Said it took them all of 24 hours to abolish it. Kath sends her apologies; she is running late, having to address after school, the Woolwich Friends of Russia meeting and lobbying Deptford Council to secure food and shelter for the Scots coming to Deptford as part of the hunger marches.

Comrade 1: With Tom Mann jailed again and, after the Battle of Deptford Bridge, our number of lead activists continues to fall as police and state are never happier than locking up our comrades . We really need a case to fight for justice in the courts. We have nothing without the law on our side, so I welcome this evening's proposal to establish the Council of Civil Liberties, but with whom and how will we take this forward?

Comrade 2: Kath will have ideas about this; we should wait until she gets here.

Kath enters

Sandy: My wife is a good woman and dedicated comrade, but she has a job-teaching over the past 27 years children that she loves and who inspire her. There is never a day when our house is not full of people seeking her help and advice, and every night there is not a meeting at which she is not speaking or mobilising the troops. There is a limit to what we can ask or impose on Kath;

to stand and fight will certainly cost her her job of 27 years and, almost certainly, her liberty.

Kath: Good evening comrades, sorry I am late, the meeting, as always, overran but catching the end of Sandy's comments, I do have more on my plate than usual, although since not getting elected for the Greenwich Parliamentary seat in the General Election for the party, I do have some time.

Fred: Kath, to take on the state, the law courts and Parliament could cost you your job and your health; you do far too much already.

Comrade 1: We need to talk about our action to mobilise workers for jobs at the local Labour Exchanges. The government have banned our stalls outside Labour Exchanges over the past years and have now brought in a ban, so any protests within 150 yards of a labour exchange risk the person being jailed. They fear that our action in mobilising the workers at the docks and so on is helping our cause in bringing about our glorious revolution.

Kath: Comrades, I have to go.

Focus shifts to Kath's House. Kath arrives home.

Mam reads from Paper

Mam: "Albert Buford from Manor Road, Brockley, has just got one month's hard labour for speaking out at the anti-Fascist rally last week and telling Mosley exactly what he thought, and telling everyone who could hear that he was a proud communist". It says here when the Judge sent him down, he gripped the dock and shouted, "Down with the fascist government, down with the fascist National Government!" as a number of police officers forcefully took him down to the cells.

So much for saying what you think! We just fought a war for them, and we still face prison for saying what we think. It's not right!

Lodger: I don't believe this. Henry has just got 12 months hard labour and his companion got 3 months at Bromley Police court.

Kath: You Mean Henry Ward, the journalist, who covers our actions from Brookmill Road.

Lodger: Yes. He and his companion, Ward, 40 years old, it says here has served 2or 3 years hard labour jail terms already. And Charles Thomas has been jailed 5 times under this antiquated law from the dark ages.

Kath: Jailed 5 times and now a further 12 months hard labour! We are talking about fighting for the right for free speech. These are just 2 gents. serving jail time for loving each other. That's it! I don't need to hear any more, I 'm off!

Kath returns to meeting, rushes in and says:

Kath: I will do it! I will lead the Labour Exchange Protests, if at the very least we establish the right for us all to have free speech. Also, the right to protest, or better still, if my arrests brings forward the Revolution, so be it.

Sandy: Are you sure, Kath? Do you realise this could be jail and the end of your career? It will be tough!

Kath: Comrades, I am blessed with a man I love and comrades I am proud to march with! What is the point of protest when you walk away from the real victory which is to bring down this unjust state? Should this not be what all comrades aspire to? I cannot continue to preach from my soap box week after week and send others to fight, if when the battle comes to me, I turn away; no comrades this is a just fight. I want more for the children that I teach! A world in which they can aspire to greater things, to say what they think and become who and what they wish to become. We won the World War with just men and women. The Russian Republic has shown us we can be united and overcome oppression! My fate is but a small price to pay!

Hands banging on table. Kath, Kath, Kath!

costs.

Month's Hard For West Ham Demonstrator

Charged with obstruction and assaulting the police, Albert Burford, of Manor Road, Brockley, was sentenced to a month's hard labour at West Ham police court yesterday.

He was arrested during the great demonstration against Mosley last Wednesday.

"I am a Communist, and proud of it," declared Burford, in the dock.

When told by Mr. St. John Morrow, the magistrate, that he would go to jail for a month with hard labour, Burford clung to the dock rails and shouted: "Down with the Fascist Government. Down with the Fascist National Government."

He was surrounded by a number of police officers and dragged forcibly from the dock.

Act 1 scene 4

Meeting in darkened community hall with comrades sitting around a table

Chairman: Comrades, we are gathered together to inform everyone of our latest campaign and what may be a terrible cost. Kath Duncan has agreed to be our champion and take on King , Parliament and the Courts as they continue to arrest and jail our comrades, Tom Mann and Lewellyn , just two of the latest to be jailed for speaking out. I am proud that we have here this evening Kath Duncan; National Unemployed Workers Movement Barrister, A Bing ; R Kidd from Council of Civil Liberties ; E Hanley from Amalgamated Engineers Union. Welcome!

The plan is that we challenge the latest Government ban that stops us from talking to workers and the unemployed outside or close to the Labour Exchanges. We have chosen The Test Centre on Nynehead Street, Deptford

Kath: I will need my box, but will seek to take my position outside the test centre come what may.

R Kidd: As this is a hugely important test case for Council of Civil Liberties, I will be present as we all in this room will be.

A Bing: I will be present to insure we can have a legal eye over the whole situation, although it is not clear if anything at all will happen, after all, they may just choose to ignore us.

Sandy: Ignore us? Our house and our meetings have been invested with Government spies for months; there is nothing we do they don't know, all that we have is our cause.

Kath: It is right that our cause is just, but comrades there must be NO violence. This is, and must be, a peaceful protest. I will chalk up around Deptford to rally support and get the word out to all our people.

E Hanley: By having our Union present, it helps to argue our case that all of us in the room are sharing a common agenda. We are calling for the right of all men and women to have free speech and the right to protest without fear of a beating or jail.

Chairman: We are agreed.

Kath: We should call the protest "SEDITION." Our Aim and objective: To defend the right of free speech and public meeting. All say aye!

Banging of table

Chairman: What we are about to do, or should I say what comrade Kath Duncan is about to do, is historic. We are challenging the power of the state, doing what is long overdue, embedding OUR civil rights; the legal right in law to free speech and protest our fair grievance. May liberty prevail!

Sound of people protesting.

People: No justice! Free our Kath! Free our Kath!

Repeat four times.

Prison Governor's office. Governor agitated at his desk just putting the phone down as a knock on his office door.

Enter Wardens.

Warden 1: Sir, there must be a good few thousand at the gate, sir; men, women and children and they're not all from the street demanding the release of Kath Duncan.

Gov: Do you think I am deaf and stupid? Every night and every morning Kath Bunkum, The Red Herring, Mrs Katherine Sinclair Duncan or whatever she likes to call herself is all I hear night and day! Whose bloody stupid idea was it to jail her?

Warden 2: She was found guilty by the courts, sir.

Gov: Yes, for not saying a bloody word, when in history have we locked up a woman rather than for fear what her words may lead to than for not saying anything? Are they not aware from Glasgow to Moscow they have turned this commie agitator into the martyr of our times, when if they wanted to silence her, chopping off her head would have been a better option.

Warden 1: This Letter has come from the TUC.

Reads Letter

The Following motion was passed at TUC tram drivers' meeting. We protest at the imprisonment of Kath Duncan...

Warden 2: This Letter has come from Educational Workers League

Reads Letter

"The National Executive Committee of the Educational Workers league protests strongly against the imprisonment of Mrs Duncan, a member of the league. It demands her immediate and unconditional release, since even on the admission of the judge himself, she was not shown to have committed any offence, but was sentenced under an act of Edward III , which makes proof unnecessary. Yours faithfully, O Osmond Hon General Secretary."

Warden 1: I think we need to be careful with this letter. 30,000 marched with her on the Gas Board demanding the end of the fuel poverty tax and they dropped it. 100,000 turned out at Hyde Park to hear her and others speak demanding jobs and an end to poverty and we cannot forget the company she keeps. It is no accident she is watched night and day by the secret service and her close friend, Fred Coperman, led the Invergorden mutiny that bought down the government, citing her as his inspiration.

Gov: What does this woman want? She looks and dresses like Mary Bloody Queen of Scots, is that what she wants? She wants to be the Last Queen of Scotland.

Warden 1: We need to tread carefully, sir. She is the most high profile political activist of our times. She has more followers and more influence than the suffragettes. Remember, every issue of our time, every grievance seems to have Mrs Kath Duncan firmly at the front. The Anti-Fascist Movement, welfare reform, slum landlords, defending Deptford market traders from the plans to gentrify the area, stopping the arms trade, marching with the miners, I could go on ...but I won't. (*Pause*) Also, the Communists buoyed by their revolution in Russia will milk Mrs Duncan and her imprisonment for all they can. They think she can be the force that triggers the revolution here in Great Britain NOW!

Warden 2: Whilst in part this is true, the Communist party was stripped of holding any party political position after she led the 30,000 protesters on the Gas works. Kath Duncan saw it as a Social justice poverty issue and risked all to fight what she saw as a further attack on the poor.

Gov: The woman clearly has friends in high places. I have just been speaking to the Minister on the telephone and he does not like the way we are treating Mrs Duncan. As far as I am concerned, the way I am treating one of MY prisoners, is my business. He has sent me over this letter from her husband.

Reads letter:

> "Dear Sir
> My wife, Mrs Kath Duncan was admitted to Holloway Prison. She was convicted under a statue of the reign of Edward III AD."

Gov: He is demanding we treat this commie agitator of a wife as a political prisoner and clearly she has high- powered friends. Winston Churchill has ensured her sentence be reduced from 12 months to just 1 month. I have been forced to look at this more closely, and sought to move it to the 3rd Division but the time this would take, or even moving to the 2nd division makes it not worth the trouble in view of the shortness of time left to serve. She has come without any order. At Bow Courts, the judge did make clear that Mr Tom Mann and co. were political prisoners, but in Mrs Duncan's case no order was made, as to why, that is for others to surmise; for now she has to be our *star* prisoner.

Warden 2: Tom Mann was seen at Bow magistrates court and was ordered to be dealt with in the district division. Kath Duncan was dealt with at Tower Magistrates court and no order was made in her case. There seems to be no grounds for approaching the magistrate with a view to making an order now, although the third division seems to show an order could be made

Warden 1: I would suggest with the minister reducing her sentence to just 1 month and with just 2 weeks to go before her release, we leave it as it is.

Warden 2: A new group of trouble makers have formed and this time it is not run or led by the Communists, the National Unemployed Workers Union, but people across the political spectrum and social classes demanding Social Justice, would you believe? They are clearly using this case with full support to establish The Council of Civil Liberties as a new pressure group.

Gov: It won't last. It's just another short term political agitation group. Who cares about the civil liberties of the poor?

Phone Rings. Governor Picks up phone. Puts down phone.

Gov: The Home Office minister has just confirmed the Council for Civil Liberties have changed their name to The National Council Of Civil Liberties, clearly intent on turning this into a test case and the first Civil rights case before the Courts, seeking to make some historic, legal point. They have just served papers at the Kings Bench: case – Duncan vs. Jones. Whilst, to throw further coals on the fire, Labour Party leader George Lansbury has just won a motion in the Houses of Parliament , calling Lloyd George and Ramsey MacDonald and the Home Office Minister to speak on Kath Duncan and Tom Mann and their Civil rights, an issue to be debated 22 December 1932.

Mark my words, jailing the most high profile "Civil Rights " activist of our times has been a huge mistake, nothing will ever be the same again, Damn this woman!

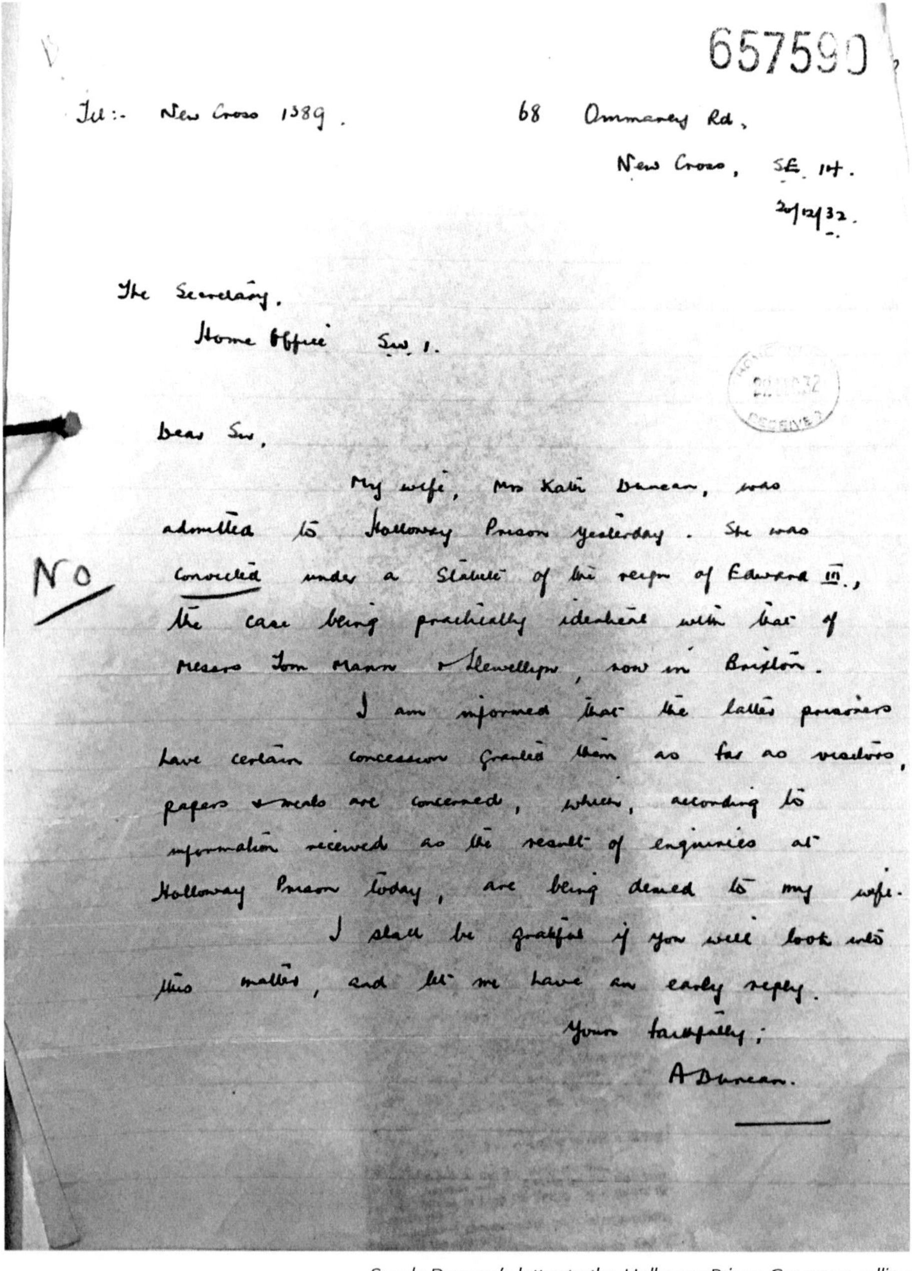

657590

Tel:- New Cross 1389.

68 Ommaney Rd,
New Cross, S.E. 14.
21/12/32.

The Secretary.
Home Office S.W. 1.

Dear Sir,

My wife, Mrs Kate Duncan, was admitted to Holloway Prison yesterday. She was convicted under a Statute of the reign of Edward III, the case being practically identical with that of Messrs Tom Mann & Llewellyn, now in Brixton.

I am informed that the latter prisoners have certain concessions granted them as far as visitors, papers & meals are concerned, which, according to information received as the result of enquiries at Holloway Prison today, are being denied to my wife.

I shall be grateful if you will look into this matter, and let me have an early reply.

Yours faithfully,

A Duncan.

NO

Sandy Duncan's letter to the Holloway Prison Governor calling for his wife to be recognised as a political prisoner

TRANSPORT AND GENERAL WORKERS' UNION

General Secretary:
ERNEST BEVIN.

Asst. General Secretary:
JOHN CLIFF.

Financial Secretary:
STANLEY HIRST.

Telegraphic Address :
" TRANSUNION PARL LONDON."

Registered Office : TRANSPORT HOUSE.
SMITH SQUARE, WESTMINSTER, S.W.1.

Telephone No. :
VICTORIA 7671.

Secretary's Address :.................................
.... 2113, New x R·
"B." .... S. E. 14

Branch
Stamp.

10 . 1 . 19 33.

Dear Sir

The following rest was
passed at meeting of above Lodge
representing 1.250 tramwaymen
held on the 6th int

We, the members of the New x
Branch of the T & J x W,
protests against the imprisonment
of Kath Duncan, & calls for
her immediate release
This rest to be forwarded
to the Home Secty.

Sir John Gilmour
"The Home Secty"

The Notes of a Spy

31st   July   4

Kath Sinclair
DUNCAN.
Police Court.

301/MP/1994.

Kath Sinclair DUNCAN, a school teacher, of
68 Ommaney Road, S.E., appeared at Tower Bridge Police
Court at 10 a.m. this day to answer a charge of "wilfully
obstructing Inspector William Jones, a constable of the
Metropolitan Police Force, whilst in the execution of his
duty, at Nynehead Street, S.E., on the 30th July, 1934,
etc".

When she stepped into the Dock she immediately
asked the Learned Magistrate — W. H. Oulton, Esq., — for
a remand to enable her to prepare her defence and obtain
legal aid.   Objection was raised by prosecuting counsel
on the grounds that the case was a simple one of obstruction
of a police officer, and that it required no elaborate
defence.   Duncan responded that she wished to call
witnesses to rebut the anticipated evidence of police and,
during the short time at her disposal since her release
on bail yesterday, she had had no time to get into touch
with them.

The Magistrate accordingly granted a remand
in Duncan's own recognisances of £5, until Monday next,
6th August, at 10.30 a.m.

I am informed that the Council for Civil
Liberties will endeavour to make this an important case
and will brief counsel for the defence.

In view, however, of the nature of the charge
which cannot truthfully be denied, it is almost certain

that a conviction will ensue.

Duncan was met outside the Court by her husband, Ronald KIDD and Ken HARVEY. Ronald KIDD, after a short consultation with Duncan, drove away in motor car Index No. Y.M.8389. The Duncans and Harvey took refreshment at a local public house and then departed by tram for Greenwich.

No attempt was made to demonstrate outside the police court, where not more than twelve persons were assembled. I have been told that, in this campaign of the N.U.W.M. against the police ban on meetings outside labour exchanges, the instructions to speakers are for them to abstain from incitement of the audience which would result in a physical clash with police.

William East.

Sergeant.

Submitted.

W. Hay.

Inspector.

[signature]

Superintendent.

EDUCATIONAL WORKERS' LEAGUE.

(FORMERLY TEACHERS' LABOUR LEAGUE; FOUNDED 1922).

English Section. Educational Workers' International, Paris.
Affiliated to the National Minority Movement, October, 1930.

Chairman: A. DUNCAN.

Vice-Chairman: A. McMILLAN.

Treasurer: Mrs. E. R. GRIFFITHS,
50, Duckett Road, Harringay,
London, N.4.

Official Organ:
"The Educational Worker," monthly 2d., or 2/6 per annum post free; Editor, 7 John St., Theobalds Rd., London, W.C.1.

Phone: Perivale 2664.

Hon. General Secretary:
C. OSMOND,
95, Fowlers Walk,
Ealing,
London, W.5.

December 31st, 1932.

To the Home Secretary,
The Home Office,
Whitehall, S.W.

Dear Sir,

The National Executive Committee of the Educational Workers' League protests strongly against the imprisionment of Mrs Duncan, a member of the League. It demands her immediate and unconditional release, since, even on the admission of the judge himself, she was not shown to have committed any offence, but was sentenced under an Act of Edward III, which makes such proof unnecessary.

Yours faithfully,

C. Osmond.

Hon. General Secretary.

UNEMPLOYED AND SLOGANS.

POLES BARRED.

Mr. A. Anderson, the chairman of the Deptford and Greenwich Unemployed, writes :—

" I want to ask for the indulgence of your Press in order to enter a public protest against the action of the police authorities against the unemployed workers in the district.

On Friday, October 16th, the unemployed workers were gathering on Deptford Broadway in preparation for a march on the County Hall, Westminster Bridge-road. As has always been the case, our unemployed workers brought with them slogans mounted on poles. What, therefore, could be their surprise when they are informed by an officer that they are to leave their slogans behind or take them off the poles and carry them in their hands!

The point I want to make is, that the unemployed were absolutely orderly, were not causing trouble in any way, but were simply gathering to march with banners and slogans to protest against their miserable conditions. Since when has it been a crime in this country to protest against starvation? Since when has there been the right to prevent unemployed workers from carrying slogans in a protest demonstration?

Do the local police intend to prevent the local Boy Scouts from carrying similar poles? Not on your life—it is only the unemployed who are to be threatened and deprived of the right to demonstrate as their forefathers demonstrated before them, with banners and slogans.

This is not a question of party politics, and I ask ' The Kentish Mercury ' to give publicity to it."

Act 2.

National Unemployed Workers' Movement (Arrests)

House of Commons. 22 December 1932.
Stage to be set to traverse, in order to represent the debating chamber. This is to give the effect that members of the audience take part in the play and become members of the House, witnessing the ensuing debate.

Speaker: Mr Lansbury.

Lansbury: The subject that I want to bring before the House is that of the case of Mr. Tom Mann and the other person who are at present detained because they refused to give sureties. Mrs. Duncan was also charged in South-East London, as well as Tom Mann and his friends. I hope that the Home Secretary will consider this matter very carefully. We are of the opinion that during the last few years – I raised this question when the right hon. Gentleman the Member for Darwen (Sir H. Samuel) was Home Secretary – that the police authorities generally and the Metropolitan Police especially have taken up an attitude towards public meetings and processions, which is, relatively speaking, new.

The start of these restrictions took place during the Home Rule discussion and during the unemployment meetings after 1886. I am quite certain that Conservative meetings, official Liberal meetings and official Labour meetings are not dealt with in this fashion. It is only what is considered to be, in the police's judgment, if you please, a sort of outside or left-wing or Communist meeting that is so dealt with. It is no business of the police to know what any of the citizens are thinking about or what they are talking about. What is it to do with them?

The police authorities in London have been permitted to assume the right to go about and discover when meetings are being held and who is going to conduct them. I attended one meeting and the police came – this was a year or two back, but it is being done now – and they wanted a list of people who were going to speak. I raised a question in the House, and I was told that no one had instructed them but that they wanted to know. I expect that there was a burglary going on round the corner, or perhaps a murder, but, instead of the police attending to their own business, they were interfering with something that was absolutely no concern of theirs.

In 1886, when there were disturbances, you could not have the sort of charge by the police that you have nowadays, when they plunge into a crowd on horseback armed with long sticks. That never happened. When there was danger of a riot, the Riot Act was read, and the people were warned to disperse. There is no warning to-day. I am speaking of what I know. No one rides along and says to the people on the pavement, "You must clear off," but they just gallop along and charge into the people. I have been ridden down myself when walking along Roman Road at Bow by patrols on the pavement, and no notice was given that we were doing anything illegal. We were just charged by the police.

I want to know why it is that the authorities have taken this power. If you compare the manner in which they disperse a Labour or Socialist crowd with their manner of dealing with a crowd which assembles to see a great wedding outside the Abbey or St. Margaret's, and which is equally a nuisance, there is a great difference. It does not matter that there is inconvenience to the general public who want to go about their business, that the road is blocked and people have to go round, and so on; the treatment is altogether different.

The Communist party and ourselves have nothing in common so far as tactics are concerned. We shall denounce any attempt to incite people to violence under any sort of conditions. However, it is the Communists to-day; it may be ourselves to-morrow. We say that because there is no sort of equality of treatment in this matter. I should like to draw the attention of the House to the fact that there is a Fascist organisation in London to-day, which makes much more seditious speeches than are made by any Communist in the country. But no one takes any notice of them; no one has yet attempted to stop the drilling of the Fascists. During one of my elections—I think it was the election before last – a set of able-bodied, well-fed, well-groomed, well-to-do young men marched through my division, for the purpose, if you please, of preserving order. I took no notice of them, because the women took them in hand and smacked their faces for them. But I am perfectly certain that, if they had been 20 or 30 Communists, in red shirts instead of black shirts, who had gone into a Tory constituency, the police would have dealt with them. This matter, really, is entirely a class business. The black-shirts in London are being organised, and they may make their speeches. I notice that hon. Gentlemen smile, but one of these days, when Mosley marches up here, they will, perhaps, smile the other way. Before I proceed, I should like to say a word about Tom Mann. I have no personal knowledge of either of the two other prisoners but Tom Mann is my friend. I know him as a man who is rather different from the ordinary agitator. He has not, from agitation, become a Member of Parliament; he has remained an agitator all his life. I do not think that that is any discredit to him; I think it is greatly to his credit.

I have never known him to advocate that unarmed men should go against armed men. He may have done what Sir Oswald Mosley is doing now, that is to say, talked about the day when the workers would probably have to fight for their rights; but I never remember him urging men to throw themselves against the police or the military. He has simply been working for poor people, and his position to-day is that he is a very poor man indeed, so that no one in this

House can stand up and charge him with being "on the make."

Hon. Members: "Hear, hear!"

Lansbury: The fact is that he is a very poor man, and he is a poor man, not because he has not brains enough to be a rich man, but because he chose to give his life in that particular way to the people to whom he belongs. Therefore, I think he is entitled to some consideration at the hands of this House. Tom Mann has never yet led a riot at a church, such as has taken place at St. Hilary, in Cornwall, within the last few weeks. Apparently the Solicitor-General does not know anything about that case. The Solicitor-General only knows about Communist agitators. The police do not trouble about such people, which shows that there is only one particular set of law-breakers that they know anything about. Why did the Solicitor General not prosecute them?

Speaker: Mr Merriman.

Merriman: The right hon. Gentleman has raised this topic and has challenged me. Will he permit me to say, first of all, that the police were present, and, secondly, that they are prosecuting?

Speaker: Mr Lansbury.

Lansbury: Yes, but you took no steps to prevent the disturbance taking place. One would have thought, when you were going to have a disturbance in the church, you would have used these powers that you are using against Tom Mann. You have not the pluck to do that, because they have very powerful friends, and you only attack those who cannot hit you back. Tom Mann has not organised a volunteer army yet; he has not imported arms into the country, and he has not yet started drilling, as do the Fascists.

Let me come to the case of Mrs. Kate Duncan. I am going to speak now with very great deference in the presence of my hon. and learned Friend and of the Solicitor-General, because I suppose this a matter of law. This woman was a disturber of the peace and an inciter of others to commit crime and, as such, subject to the provisions of the Statute of 34 Edward III. What is this Statute? I was a victim of it. You may have this lady in the House as well as myself one of these days and, having been prosecuted, she may even speak from this Box. Here is the sort of thing that this Act was passed to deal with. Last year this same public Department had great trouble in dealing with the opening of cinemas and such places on Sunday because of a silly old law, and everyone stood up and said, "These laws ought to be swept away." Of all the tomfool laws to apply in modern times, this one takes the biscuit. That in every county of England shall be assigned for the keeping of the peace, one lord, and with him three or four of the most worthy in the county, with some learned in the law, and they shall have power to restrain the offenders, rioters, and all other barrators and to pursue, arrest, take, and chastise them according to their trespass or offence. Of course, now you are not allowed to chastise them. I should like to see you start chastising them. It means that you can flog them before you imprison them: and to cause them to be imprisoned and duly punished according to the law and customs of the realm. There is no law and custom now to allow the police to chastise anyone.

Speaker: Mr Holford Knight.

Knight: It is all obsolete.

Speaker: Mr Lansbury.

Lansbury: This is the Act under which they are put away.

Speaker: Mr Holford Knight.

Knight: A historical document.

Speaker: Mr Lansbury.

Lansbury: It reads like a novel and an ancient one at that— and to inquire of all those that have been pillors and robbers in the parts beyond the sea"— Is it charged against Tom Mann and Mrs. Duncan that they are robbers across the sea and be now come again and go wandering?" – Tom Mann has a residence. He does not wander. He is not a vagrant. and will not labour" – There is no charge against him that he will not labour. He is six years older than the old age pension age and he has committed no crime. However, he was an engineer. The judges, on the other hand said, "This chap has to be put away and put away he must be." I do not think I need read any more. I suggest that this would be good bedtime reading for anyone who really wants to see the kind of law under which Communists and other people are dealt with. You only deal with Communists and common people under this law. You dare not bring it into operation against the Mosleyites. No one can deny that. It is only poor people. Mrs. Kate Duncan was charged. Let us see the evidence that she was a killer, a robber, a wanderer and a vagabond, and that she had done something she ought not to have done. The right hon. Gentleman may have a longer report of the case. I am only able to quote from the report in the "Times." Mr Clayton, the solicitor, said that in a speech in Bermondsey Town Hall Mrs Duncan spoke in a manner calculated to create a breach of the peace. Mr Clayton said that he thought that Duncan was then speaking about a Bermondsey murder case. What right has he to pretend to say what he thought? What a solicitor thinks is not evidence, however distinguished he may be.

Hon. Member: "Hear, hear."

Lansbury: Mr. Clayton said that her words were calculated to provoke a breach of the peace. But wait a minute, Detective Inspector Jones, of the Special Branch, said that he was at the meeting in question and heard Duncan use certain words alleged. He did not take a shorthand note. He made a note soon afterwards. There never had been a shorthand note taken. Further police reports have Duncan present at other demonstrations at Peckham and at Camberwell Town Hall, where filthy and insulting words were used. The point is that there is not a scrap of evidence that the woman used any alleged filthy language, but in the report in *The Times* there is not a word of evidence that this woman used this language at all. This is how the Press reports a poor woman. Duncan, in a long rambling speech, denied that she had used any insulting words or conduct likely to provoke a breach of the peace. There is not a scrap of definite evidence against the woman. She gave her own version of the case, and Mr. Campion, the magistrate, said that he would be willing to take Duncan's word. That shows the impression which the woman and the evidence had made upon the magistrate. He said that he would take her word that no such conduct would happen again, and would bind her over in her own recognisances to keep the peace for six months. Mrs. Duncan said "What if I refuse?" and Mr. Campion said, "You will have to find a surety of £50." Mrs. Duncan: "I do not want any surety." This woman was in the same position. I call the attention of the Home Secretary to the fact that the magistrate was willing to let her off on her word without any sureties at all unless this report is wrong. I will read it again: He would be willing to take Duncan's word that no such conduct would happen again.

Speaker: Mr Stanley

Stanley: Read the next few words.

Lansbury: All right. "That no such conduct would happen again".

Stanley: The next few words.

Lansbury: When she refused to find sureties she was ordered to go to prison for a month in default. Unless the right hon. Gentleman has some evidence which is not given in the report in the "Times," I say that there is no evidence against the woman. It is not worth the paper that it is written on. I should like the Home Secretary or the Solicitor-General to give us some reason why the woman cannot be released forthwith and allowed to go free.

When we come to the case of Tom Mann and his friend it is a little complicated because of the Act of 1817. Here is what Mr. Wallace said for the prosecution: He would ask that the accused men be ordered to enter into their own recognisances and to find surety or sureties for their future good behaviour and to keep the peace. The court had power to make such an order under a very old Act, the Act of Edward III, and the Seditious Meetings Act, 1817 which said that meetings of more than 50 persons within a mile of Westminster, during the sitting of Parliament or of the Superior Courts, for the purpose or on the pretext of considering or preferring a petition, complaint, remonstrance or address to the King, or either House of Parliament, for alterations in matters of Church or State, were deemed to be unlawful assemblies. I would point out that part of that Act is already obsolete. The Courts of Justice were formerly alongside Westminster Hall and were part of this building. Now they are situated in the Strand, and any procession at any time can go past the Law Courts. I came past the Law Courts with a great procession when the Poplar councillors were tried. We were escorted through the City of London and treated quite properly by the authorities. We marched right up to the courts. Nobody thinks now of stopping a procession simply because it is passing the Law Courts, but this Act says that you must not take a procession past the Law Courts.

I am advised that unlawful assembly – I hope the Home Secretary will pay attention to this point—does not constitute a breach of the peace. Therefore, whatever the charge was against these men it could not be a charge concerning a breach of the peace. Unlawful assembly is mentioned in the, Act of 1817. Therefore the right hon. Gentleman must prove something more than was proven at the court. Mr. Wallace went on to say: The accused men were well known members of the Communist party" – It is a matter of agreement between us that to be a, member of the Communist party is not something illegal. I should, however, like to ask the Home Secretary a question on that point so that that position may be affirmed. Membership of the Communist party or of the National Committee of the Unemployed is not illegal. They have not been proclaimed illegal organisations. In the 5th December issue of the 'Daily Worker,' the organ of the Communist party, there was an article which began: Unemployed! Call for action on 20th December. Fight for petition to be presented to Parliament. I have written that sort of thing many times. It does not necessarily mean that you are going to fight in any other sense than we fight one another across this piece of oak furniture. The right hon. Gentleman has to prove that these men were guilty of inciting people to do something that was unlawful. They have done nothing of the kind. There is nothing in that article which incites anybody to do anything that is illegal, and the right hon. Gentleman knows that as well as I do. There is not_a scrap of evidence to show that Tom Mann or Llewellyn ever wrote that article or were employed on the "Daily Worker." There is not a scrap of evidence that they had any connection whatsoever with it. You might as well say that I am responsible for what appears in the "Daily Herald" because I am a member of a party –

Speaker: Mr Buchanan.

Buchanan: They are bad enough, but they would not go to that length.

Speaker: Mr Lansbury.

Lansbury: Because Tom Mann is a member of the Communist party he cannot be held responsible for what every writer in the "Daily Worker" writes. Tom Mann is not the editor of the "Daily Worker". There is no evidence that he or Llewellyn wrote the article or had anything to do with it. There is nothing else against them except that in some way they are linked up with this article. I challenge the right hon. Gentleman to prove any connection other than that they were members of the Communist party, and that they were officials of the National Unemployed Workers Society. On 9th December a letter headed "The National Unemployed Workers' Movement, the National Administrative Council" – those are not very revolutionary words – was delivered to the Prime Minister at the House of Commons. It described the officials as Mr. Elias, Mr. Wal Hannington as the organiser, Mr. Tom Mann as the treasurer, and Mr. Llewellyn as the secretary. The letter was as follows: Following our request prior to Tuesday, 1st November, to you and the Speaker of the House to allow a deputation of the unemployed and employed representatives to present a petition to which we have one million signatures, and also to allow this representative delegation to state their views before the House, we are going to make a similar request that you meet this deputation on 19th December. The deputation will also present the million signatures petition. It is our opinion that the Government, and particularly yourself as responsible head of the Government, should have regard to the views of over one million people in this country who have signed this national petition, which we desire to present and await your reply to this request. What is there illegal in that? I should have thought it was a respectable, courteous and gentlemanly letter, written in the best Oxford and Cambridge style. I want someone to tell me any particular sentence in this letter which is illegal. Mr. Wallace, in his submission, said that the letter clearly connected the National Unemployed Workers Movement with the publication in the "Daily Worker," and that the people responsible were Mann and Llewellyn. Is there a shred of evidence of any connection between the two? I have read what the "Daily Worker" said. They called for mass action, a gathering of the unemployed, not specifying where, and this letter was written asking the Prime Minister to receive a deputation. The representatives of people who are suffering as the unemployed ought to be heard. They represent a considerable feeling in this country, and they have a petition which they say is signed by one million persons. They have a right to bring that petition to the House and to ask for permission to present it, although the House can deny them the right to come to the Bar of the House. But there is nothing criminal in all this. Mr Wallace in his speech went on to say: It is well known, from what has happened on former occasions, what is likely to happen when large numbers of unemployed and other people as well get together on instructions to present petitions to Parliament. The Government base their action on what happened in November; once bitten twice shy, these people called a demonstration and attempted to get into the House. But see what happened on this occasion—and what right have you to assume that it would not have happened with Tom Mann. Detective Passmore gave evidence as to what happened at the last demonstration, but there is no evidence that Mr. Mann was there and no evidence was given that his friend was there. They are mere statements, no evidence at all. Tom Mann made his speech, and this is what he said—there is not a scrap of evidence to contravert it – He did not participate in violence but merely took part in meetings which were admittedly within the right of citizens. He held that these proceedings were entirely unwarranted. He looked upon them as part of the general procedure of the authorities against the workers' committee. His aim and object had been to get legitimate grievances remedied in a fair, straightforward honest and becoming fashion. Llewellyn addressed the magistrate in the same way. He said: No violence had ever been advocated by him, and what violence had taken place was against innocent demonstrators. That is all the evidence. Then he went on: There is nothing to prevent anyone presenting a petition to the House of Commons, but it is most undesirable that such a petition should be presented by an organised mass of people marching on the House of Commons. Certainly, but there is no evidence to show that Tom Mann and Llewellyn had any such intention, and my case is that unless you can prove that intention you had no right to arrest. I may be a very ignorant person, but until Tom Mann was arrested I had no knowledge whatever that this demonstration was to be held, and I believe that the arrest of Tom Mann gave all the publicity that the Communist party desired; it gave the meeting just the advertisement that it wanted.

Speaker: Mr Buchanan.

Buchanan: In connection with the case against Mrs. Duncan I am not a lawyer, but I think I know just a little about it. Hitherto, in the courts which I have attended – and I have watched some of the so-called worst criminals being tried – I have constantly watched the judge being fair to the defence. In Scotland we lay it down that it is the Procurator's duty not to prosecute, but to see that the facts are brought out. The trial of that woman would never have been tolerated in any court if the charge had only been ordinary theft, or even a grave charge of murder. The whole thing was done in an atmosphere of sentence before trial. I hope the Home Secretary will say that he thinks this prosecution was mistakenly undertaken, and that the trial of Mrs. Duncan was not conducted in a way that did credit to law and justice in this country. I hope that, as Home Secretary, he will take the necessary action to overturn those decisions and that he will act a manly part, not only for his own sake and for the sake of his office, but above all for the sake of giving justice a decent name in this country.

Speaker: Mr Gilmour.

Gilmour: The last thing I should desire to do would be to introduce any heat into this discussion, but I must join issue at once when he asks me to say that the trial which was conducted in dealing with Mrs. Duncan was improperly done, or that there was distinct unfairness on the part of Mr. Wallace. I would say frankly that this is not the place in which trials before courts should be reviewed. It is most unsuitable, and I suppose that at any rate it will be recognised that men like Mr. Wallace, who have these grave responsibilities, have every right to be protected against assertions to which they cannot reply. Whether it be this case or the cases of Tom Mann and Llewellyn, I want to bring the House back to the position in which any officer in any executive position stands who has to deal with these problems at the present time. I for the time being occupy this post, and I want to assure the House of Commons, and any who may be critics of what I may do, that the one thing above all which I desire to avoid is to allow circumstances to develop into a position in which I shall require to use the forces at my disposal and not only involve my executive and my officers in grave risks, but bring about a conflict and a clash of forces in the streets of this metropolis which can only end in bringing disaster to many people, not only those who are guilty of incitement, but those who in many cases are the dupes of those people. With regard to the case of Tom Mann and Llewellyn: Let me put this to the House. This particular case was taken through the proper channels. The defendants were brought to the court, and, as far as I know, they never denied that there was justification for their being brought into court. What they refused to do there was to give a plain and perfectly simple undertaking that they would not carry out what the law said they ought not to do.

Speaker: Mr McEntee.

McEntee: They were not charged with that.

Speaker: Mr Gilmour.

Gilmour: Of course, they were not accused of that, but it was made clear that all they were asked was that they would behave themselves as orderly citizens of this country.

Speaker: Mr Lansbury.

Lansbury: The point is, the right hon. Gentleman has built up his case against these two men on what happened previously. The magistrate himself said that he did not hold these two men responsible for what happened in November.

Speaker: Mr Gilmour.

Gilmour: Whether that was so or not, the whole position is this: that if we had a repetition of what happened before it was going to lead to very grave disorders. In an endeavour to prevent it these men are asked to give undertakings that they will not incite or take part in any such disorderly proceedings. Is it too much to ask?

Hon. Members: "Yes!"

Gilmour: They refused to do it, and they have suffered the consequences. In both cases I have no reason to think that justice has not been carried out, and I do not propose to release them.

Speaker: Mr Maxton.

Maxton: What about Mrs Duncan?

Speaker: Mr Lloyd George.

Lloyd George: I do not propose to continue the exhaustive discussion, which has been carried on during the last few hours.

The Red Flag

The people's flag is deepest red,
It shrouded oft our martyred dead,
And ere their limbs grew stiff and cold,
Their hearts' blood dyed its ev'ry fold.

> Then raise the scarlet standard high.
> Within its shade we'll live and die,
> Though cowards flinch and traitors sneer,
> We'll keep the red flag flying here.

Look 'round, the Frenchman loves its blaze,
The sturdy German chants its praise,
In Moscow's vaults its hymns are sung
Chicago swells the surging throng.

> Then raise the scarlet standard high.
> Within its shade we'll live and die,
> Though cowards flinch and traitors sneer,
> We'll keep the red flag flying here.

It waved above our infant might,
When all ahead seemed dark as night;
It witnessed many a deed and vow,
We must not change its colour now.

> Then raise the scarlet standard high.
> Within its shade we'll live and die,
> Though cowards flinch and traitors sneer,
> We'll keep the red flag flying here.

It well recalls the triumphs past,
It gives the hope of peace at last;
The banner bright, the symbol plain,
Of human right and human gain.

      Then raise the scarlet standard high.
      Within its shade we'll live and die,
      Though cowards flinch and traitors sneer,
      We'll keep the red flag flying here.

It suits today the weak and base,
Whose minds are fixed on pelf and place
To cringe before the rich man's frown,
And haul the sacred emblem down.

      Then raise the scarlet standard high.
      Within its shade we'll live and die,
      Though cowards flinch and traitors sneer,
      We'll keep the red flag flying here.

With heads uncovered swear we all
To bear it onward till we fall;
Come dungeons dark or gallows grim,
This song shall be our parting hymn.

      Then raise the scarlet standard high.
      Within its shade we'll live and die,
      Though cowards flinch and traitors sneer,
      We'll keep the red flag flying here.

Written: 1889
Lyrics: Jim Connel

1935
Oct. 16.

DUNCAN *v.* JONES.

Police—Public meeting in street—Reasonable apprehension of breach of the peace—Right to prohibit.

The appellant was about to address a number of people in a street when a police officer, who reasonably apprehended that a breach of the peace would occur if the meeting were held, forbade her to do so. The appellant persisted in trying to hold the meeting and obstructed the police officer in his attempts to prevent her doing so. Neither the appellant nor any of the persons present at the meeting committed, incited, or provoked a breach of the peace :—

Held, that, as it is the duty of a police officer to prevent breaches of the peace which he reasonably apprehends, the appellant was guilty of wilfully obstructing the officer when in the execution of his duty.

CASE stated by County of London Quarter Sessions.

At 1 P.M. on July 30, 1934, about thirty people, including the appellant, Mrs. Katherine Duncan, collected with a view to holding a meeting in Nynehead Street, New Cross, in the borough of Deptford, near to the entrance to an unemployed training centre situate in that street. At the entrance to Nynehead Street a notice was written across the roadway as follows :—

(1) On Dec. 2, 1935, leave to appeal to the House of Lords was granted to the defendant.

"SEDITION."

Meeting at the Test Centre to-day (now) 1 P.M.

Speakers : R. Kidd (Council for Civil Liberties),

A. Bing (Barrister-at-Law),

E. Hanley (Amalgamated Engineers' Union),

K. Duncan (National Unemployed

Workers' Movement),

Defend the right of free speech and public meeting.

A box was placed in the roadway opposite the entrance to the training centre, on which the appellant was about to mount, when the chief constable of the district, with whom was the respondent, William Jones, an inspector of the Metropolitan Police, told the appellant that a meeting could not be held in Nynehead Street, but that it could be held in Desmond Street, some 175 yards distant. The appellant then said : " I'm going to hold it," stepped on to the box, and started to address the people who were present, when the respondent immediately took her into custody, to which she submitted without resistance.

An information was preferred on August 6, 1934, at Tower Bridge Police Court by the respondent against the appellant under the Prevention of Crimes Act, 1871, s. 12, as amended by the Prevention of Crimes Amendment Act, 1885, s. 2, alleging that on July 30, 1934, the appellant did unlawfully and wilfully obstruct the respondent when in the execution of his duty. The magistrate convicted the appellant and fined her 40s. The appellant appealed to London Quarter Sessions.

At the hearing of the appeal it was not alleged on behalf of the respondent that there was any obstruction of the highway or of the access to the training centre, save in the sense of the obstruction necessarily caused by the box which was placed in the roadway and by the presence of the people surrounding it. Neither was it alleged that the appellant nor any of the persons present at the meeting had either committed, incited or provoked any breach of the peace.

S 2

It was proved or admitted that on May 25, 1933, a meeting had been held opposite the entrance to the training centre, and the appellant had addressed that meeting. Following that meeting and on the same day a disturbance took place inside the training centre. The superintendent of the training centre, who attributed the disturbance to the meeting, sent for the police to prevent a breach of the peace. Subsequently, and in spite of the disturbance and of warnings by the police, the appellant, for some reason unexplained by her, made one or more attempts to hold a meeting at the same spot, which were frustrated by the police. Before July 30, 1934, the superintendent of the training centre, who feared a repetition of the previous disturbance, communicated with the police, and by reason of such communication and of reports by the police in the course of their duty, the chief constable of the district and the respondent apprehended that a breach of the peace would result if the meeting now in question were held.

The deputy-chairman of quarter sessions was of opinion : (1.) that in fact (if it be material) the appellant must have known of the probable consequences of her holding the meeting—namely, a disturbance and possibly a breach of the peace—and was not unwilling that such consequences should ensue ; (2.) that in fact the respondent reasonably apprehended a breach of the peace ; (3.) that in law it thereupon became his duty to prevent the holding of the meeting ; and (4.) that in fact, by attempting to hold the meeting, the appellant obstructed the respondent when in the execution of his duty. The appeal was, therefore, dismissed.

On the application of the appellant, quarter sessions stated this case for the opinion of the Court whether there was evidence on which the deputy-chairman could so decide in point of law.

Pritt K.C. and *Dingle Foot* for the appellant. It is not unlawful to hold a public meeting on the highway. The police have no right to prevent a person doing a lawful act merely because they think that a breach of the peace may result from it, and, therefore, when the appellant obstructed the respondent, as admittedly she did, he was not acting " in the execution of his duty " within the meaning of the statutes. In *Beatty* v. *Gillbanks* (1) the appellants assembled for a lawful purpose, but with good reason to suppose that a breach of the peace would result, yet it was held that they could not be convicted of unlawful assembly. True that the charge is different in the present case, but the same principle should be applied. On the facts stated in the present case the appellant could no more be rightly convicted than a person can be bound to good behaviour without being guilty of misbehaviour : *Reg.* v. *Londonderry Justices*, per O'Brien J. (2) If (which is not admitted) the disturbance of May, 1933, resulted from the meeting which she had then just held, she was not responsible for those who caused it, and the bad conduct of another person cannot make that wrong which is otherwise innocent. (2)

[They also referred to Dicey's Law of the Constitution, 8th ed., p. 508.]

Montgomery K.C. and *Vernon Gattie* for the respondent. If a police officer reasonably apprehends that the action of any person may result in a breach of the peace, it is his duty to prevent that action. If the appellants in *Beatty* v. *Gillbanks* (1) had been directed to discontinue the assembly by a police officer who reasonably apprehended that a breach of the peace would result, and they had refused to do so, they would have been rightly convicted of obstructing the police officer when in the execution of his duty. In *Reg.* v. *Prebble* (3) it is made clear that the police would have been justified in clearing the public-house in question of the persons assembled there " had there been . . . . any danger of a breach of the peace." (4)

[They were stopped.]

Pritt K.C. replied.

LORD HEWART C.J. There have been moments during the argument in this case when it appeared to be suggested

(1) (1882) 9 Q. B. D. 308.   (3) (1858) 1 F. & F. 325.
(2) (1891) 28 L. R. Ir. 440, 450.   (4) Ibid. per Bramwell B., at p. 326.

that the Court had to do with a grave case involving what is called the right of public meeting. I say " called," because English law does not recognize any special right of public meeting for political or other purposes. The right of assembly, as Professor Dicey puts it (1), is nothing more than a view taken by the Court of the individual liberty of the subject. If I thought that the present case raised a question which has been held in suspense by more than one writer on constitutional law—namely, whether an assembly can properly be held to be unlawful merely because the holding of it is expected to give rise to a breach of the peace on the part of persons opposed to those who are holding the meeting—I should wish to hear much more argument before I expressed an opinion. This case, however, does not even touch that important question.

Our attention has been directed to the somewhat unsatisfactory case of *Beatty* v. *Gillbanks*. (2) The circumstances of that case and the charge must be remembered, as also must the important passage in the judgment of Field J., in which Cave J. concurred. Field J. said (3) : " I entirely concede that every one must be taken to intend the natural consequences of his own acts, and it is clear to me that if this disturbance of the peace was the natural consequence of acts of the appellants they would be liable, and the justices would have been right in binding them over. But the evidence set forth in the case does not support this contention ; on the contrary, it shows that the disturbances were caused by other people antagonistic to the appellants, and that no acts of violence were committed by them." Our attention has also been directed to other authorities where the judgments in *Beatty* v. *Gillbanks* (2) have been referred to, but they do not carry the matter any further, although they more than once express a doubt about the exact meaning of the decision. In my view, *Beatty* v. *Gillbanks* (2) is apart from the present case. No such question as that which arose there is even mooted here.

(1) Dicey's Law of the Constitution, 8th ed., p. 499.

(2) 9 Q. B. D. 308.
(3) Ibid. 314.

1935
DUNCAN
v.
JONES.
———
Lord Hewart
C.J.

The present case reminds one rather of the observations of Bramwell B. in *Reg.* v. *Prebble* (1), where, in holding that a constable, in clearing certain licensed premises of the persons thereon, was not acting in the execution of his duty, he said : " It would have been otherwise had there been a nuisance or disturbance of the public peace, or any danger of a breach of the peace."

The case stated which we have before us indicates clearly a causal connection between the meeting of May, 1933, and the disturbance which occurred after it—that the disturbance was not only post the meeting but was also propter the meeting. In my view, the deputy-chairman was entitled to come to the conclusion to which he came on the facts which he found and to hold that the conviction of the appellant for wilfully obstructing the respondent when in the execution of his duty was right. This appeal should, therefore, be dismissed.

HUMPHREYS J. I agree. I regard this as a plain case. It has nothing to do with the law of unlawful assembly. No charge of that sort was even suggested against the appellant. The sole question raised by the case is whether the respondent, who was admittedly obstructed, was so obstructed when in the execution of his duty.

It does not require authority to emphasize the statement that it is the duty of a police officer to prevent apprehended breaches of the peace. Here it is found as a fact that the respondent reasonably apprehended a breach of the peace. It then, as is rightly expressed in the case, became his duty to prevent anything which in his view would cause that breach of the peace. While he was taking steps so to do he was wilfully obstructed by the appellant. I can conceive no clearer case within the statutes than that.

SINGLETON J. On the facts stated in the case I am satisfied that the respondent at the material time was doing that which it was his duty to do, and that, therefore, the obstruction

(1) 1 F. & F. 325, 326.

1935

DUNCAN

v.

JONES.

Singleton J.

of him by the appellant constituted obstruction of him when in the execution of his duty. Authorities in other branches of the law do not carry the matter any further. I agree that the appeal should be dismissed.

Appeal dismissed.

Solicitor for appellant : *R. W. G. Mackay.*
Solicitors for respondent : *Wontner & Sons.*

G. F. L. B.

Ghaffey, Mrs. Hecker, Mrs. Proctor, Mrs. Berryman, Mrs. Prosser, Mrs. Cudmore, Mrs. Glaisher, Mrs. Dallow and Miss Richmond.

KATH DUNCAN'S RELEASE.

" RECEPTION " ARRANGED.

Mrs. Kath Duncan, the Greenwich and Deptford Communist leader, will be released from Holloway Goal on Wednesday. A number of her women supporters will be at the gates when she leaves and they will escort her to Deptford, where " Kath " will address a meeting of the " comrades " in the Broadway.

In the evening she will be welcomed back at a social gathering to be held at the Greenwich Baths Hall.

PLUMSTEAD DEATH AFTER ACCIDENT.

Harry George Shearman (72), of

EPILOGUE
Speaker comes forward

On 14 August, 1954, Kath Duncan died from TB, which she contracted whilst serving time in Holloway Prison. Thousands came out onto the streets of Deptford in her honour and the word went out, "How do we toast our Comrade who did so much for every man, woman, child here today?"

A voice rang out:
> "To The Last Queen of Scotland ... Yeah, that will be the toast. To our Kath; The Last Queen of Scotland!"

Pause

> In 1957, a young black woman from the West Indies arrived in Deptford and would set about carrying on the work left by Kath Duncan's void, helping the poor and those most in need.

> Today, this awesome community activist and inspiring worker, Barbara Raymond, 80, a mother figure to many, still carries on her work in Deptford.

> In Ashton-Under-Lyne, a single mum, Charlotte Hughes, leads a nationally recognised protest outside her job centre every week, against the impact of welfare reforms on those most vulnerable and in need.

> Across the UK, the disabled have a champion in Paula Peters, who has mobilised and inspired disabled people out of their bedrooms and into taking direct action across the UK.

The women who led our struggles; the women who paid such a huge price; the women who have not come from the aristocracy or the ruling classes, deserve our respect and our solidarity. No longer must we allow the heroes of our times, like Kath Duncan, to be erased from history. She won for us all, the right to protest and the right for free speech. The National Council of Civil Liberties is now known internationally as' Liberty'. Thanks, Kath, but the struggle goes on!

Sandy Duncan died of Cancer 1942 and Mam, Kath's Mum died aged 90 in Hampstead 1952.

Raises fist in the air in sign of solidarity

The ghost of Kath Duncan appears singing the Red Flag, and as she does so every member of the cast joins in and the audience are encouraged to take part as well.

The words for the Red Flag could be on a programme or on banner or screen at front of stage.

I hope you have not forgotten the Marrows in the Cellar? In the window in Hut I have a pot of little bulbs, they will require water and air.

I suppose lil Joey is alright and Robin is

When you write dont omit to send my love to Tony

Hope you are keeping warm and well, I was very glad to see Tom & Charly. Love to Nellie, Alma & Doris

Fond love to yourself

Tom.

Pyjamas and Vest but vest new. Vest & pants. Thick shirt. Stockings. one hanky.

Letters from Tom Mann To MAM Kath Duncan's mother about Kath's poor health from Brixton Prison in which he was held the same time as Kath

Dear Mam, I hope your finger is better. I fear brother George is not likely to last long as for ...shers message. Will you please let Harry Know. I shall very much like to see them if he can manage it, if he cannot ask him to write.

We have just done half the term to day... the second half, four weeks and three days— Thursday the 16th Feb. I am quite well, am glad you brought the under jacket, I wanted it but forgot it. On next... next Friday week, I should like to see Peggy, John, Alma Nellie whichever two of these can most conveniently accompany you, but let me know early enough next week to get the order sent.

This evening you will be at Whitefields and may meet old friends.

So there has been an earthquake shock which affected Grassington? Those old Kynsleck hills seem to be slipping about. Dont omit to give my regards to all at Moorside please.

Kate Duncan will be released this week I think. I hope she has a restful spell now. I am sure she needs it. She has been looking very pale and worn for months, she undertakes too much, but she is a fine worker, please give her my hearty greetings if you see her. Also to Duly her hubby if you meet.

Next week it will be Wally's turn to reach home, the 26th I think. He too looks paler than he should. I think he is liable to an occasional break down & ought to be medically examined at once, for, myself, I have neither ache or pain.

Please give my kind regards to Mrs Reeves and her little one Posty—they are sure to be talking of me and I would like them to know I think kindly of them. If I could I would of course write to Cousin May, Aunt Soph, Ealing, Rutland Boynton and many others, but of course I may not. I see there is to be an evening for Rutlands Chamber Music, I hope it is a real Success.